REGINALD MCKIVER

THE BAGGAGE YOU UNPACKED

A GUIDE TO FINDING YOUR TRUTH

ISBN Paperback: 978-1-7364739-0-0

ISBN E-book: 978-1-7364739-1-7

CONTENTS

1

THIS BAG OF MINE DEFINED

I want you to watch people. I want you to watch them as they walk throughout life. Put yourself in the middle of this shopping plaza. All around you, you see people. You see them laughing. You see them interacting with one another. They are going on about their day. Some of them are arguing with others. There's a lady over there who's wearing makeup. She has a purse and the latest shoes, but even with all of the newest fashion, you can still sense her insecurity as she continuously checks herself, always stopping to look in the mirror as if some strand is out of place.

As you look on, you see a person who sits in a corner and just observes everyone— afraid to walk through the center of the mall because they're worried that all eyes will be on them, so they hide within the shadows. You hear someone else being loud. They talk a lot, but with no understanding, speaking, and going on and on about themselves as if to convince themselves that they have worth. You look over to your left, and there's a person who's avoiding you. They have a look on their face that shows they don't want to be bothered. They don't want to engage with life. They only want to go about their business, so they wear this look on their face that screams—if you bother me, there will be consequences.

Then you look at the playful ones. The ones who walk through that mall and throughout life as if nothing bothers them. They walk as if they have a light, but even within that light, you can see where they're holding themselves back. They're going from person to person saying, "See me, am I worthy? Am I good enough?" You look at one woman who's walking with a man. She has dressed the part, but you can still see a look of unhappiness on her face. As you're sitting there, you see yet another couple, but their relationship seems void and dead; and so, they're just generating smiles, but those smiles look as if they're hiding pain.

All around you, you begin to notice something. You begin

to notice a world where everyone is wearing a costume. Everyone is pretending to be something, but what if we could walk around this same mall and see people begin to live in their truth? You would see people with full happiness shining from the inside— holding their children; talking to their children; spending time with their children— engaging with their partner and looking into their eyes and seeing love. For the first time, instead of just hearing them talk about love, you would finally see it. Each generation after them would be better than the age before. You would see wholeness. No one would have to tell you that this is how wholeness looks. You would know this wholeness—see this fullness, and it would be self-explanatory. You'd see this glowing. A glowing that's so bright on the inside that you'd know that these people are walking within their gifts.

Why is it that we don't see this, and it's few and far between when we do? As we look at life today, as we look at Facebook or Instagram, we begin to see a world of people who put themselves out there and want attention. They want someone to accept them. They want someone to feel good with them, and the truth is, they'll never get that because they don't feel good within themselves. When you don't feel right or true within yourself, you begin to look for validation from anywhere.

Everyone looks for attention; they seek to be accepted, but no one searches for purpose. Think about your life. Think about where you sit right now— not only where you are but also your life results. When you look at the effects of what is in your life right now, nine times out of ten if you could trade it— if you could give it back, you would. Some of us have lost our identities so much that we're sitting in a place where we have limited understanding and limited belief in ourselves. We know that we're settling, yet we cannot identify for what. All we know is that there's something inside of us that keeps calling us, though a small voice in the back of our head— it's still calling us saying that there's higher inside of you. There's something there—there's a life there that you're running parallel to, but you're experiencing a polarity in this life, which is not happiness.

When we go back to the mall, we look at each person as they carry baggage. They hold a system of beliefs. They bring so many things in this bag that cause them to lose the reality of who they are meant to be. You, my friend, are sitting in the middle of the world of great performances where you watch people perform, but they're not living. Now, I want to stop right here and ask you a question.

QUESTION:

What baggage are you carrying that's sabotaging
your interactions with others?

This baggage that we take from relationship to relationship.
We are good at saying this person wasn't right for me, and
we always blame the other person. We resort to, "Well, they
cheated on me" or "They did this to me" or "I always went
through this or that!" Let's stop and look at the baggage
you're bringing to every appointment, every relationship,
and everything that comes into your life.

Now, think about this: All that you are when you shut your
eyes is a collection of thoughts, a group of belief systems.
Some of us, even with our eyes closed, begin to feel hurt
and pain. We begin to feel wounded, and sometimes when
our eyes are closed and we're alone with our thoughts, it
seems like the worst place to be—never wanting to be alone.
We never want to sit by ourselves because we know the
moment we sit by ourselves; all of these thoughts will release
through the mind that we have not dealt with. Being stored
in the body's energy systems, held in the heart, and stored
in the lungs and kidneys, housing our fears and housing our

unresolved issues. We go from person to person carrying these unresolved issues. That's not what society teaches us. Society teaches us that we're who we are, and we bring people in and out of our lives looking until we find the right person, but I ask you this: if you're not the right person for yourself, how can you be the right person for the one who is to come into your life?

I want you to do what you may have never done before. I want you to take your baggage out and look at it and see what exactly it is you're carrying from relationship to relationship— and how did it get there? From what has it grown? Think about your last relationship. How did it end? Did it end in infidelity? Did it end in self-destruction? Think about your marriage even if you're currently married— what baggage do you have in your union that you just built the relationship on top of and drew your battle lines and you stopped at those battle lines and began to create a life— "As long as you don't cross this line. As long as you don't do this, we're okay." But what if your whole marriage and your entire relationship were fake? What if your relationships were just a result of what settled with your baggage?

You have to take time to pause and think about it. Whenever you get into that relationship, you begin to unpack your bags. Everything is going well. There's a honeymoon phase. You've met them. You're so in love. You're so happy. You're introducing them to parents, and the next thing you know, they do something, or they've said something, and what happens at that point is that the words they stated begin to trigger something that someone else said before. All of these emotions start to come out. These emotions become fear; they become other things. You have your first argument, and that argument blows up, and then it blows over, but yet it has uprooted something within you before you can do anything about it. You've put a guard around your heart, and now you go on and try to make the relationship better, but then another offense comes up and triggers something else that you had in the bag. Maybe they said you were gaining weight, and you had a negative self-image in the bag about yourself. Now that they've said it, although they were just joking, it triggered something on the inside of you that meant something more profound. Now, you're altered. You're changing. Now, you're trying to stay thin. You're trying to keep in shape. Now, you're trying to stay something, but all that happened was the same thing beginning to regurgitate itself; and when it repeats itself, you lose the essence of yourself. But, what if you never had yourself? What if you never owned yourself because what was going on inside you had taken the real you away a long time ago? Now, you're going through this relationship again. Now, you've had your second argument- your third argument. Now, everything is unpacked, and the last relationship is released into this one. This relationship begins to go downhill. Have you ever thought about this? This relationship was over before it ever started. You're just maintaining time until the relationship ends because somewhere in your baggage, you've already brought "I'm not good enough for this. I'm not worthy of this, and I don't deserve this". Everywhere you go and everything you're doing in life, you're unpacking baggage.

Let's take this baggage to the job. I sit at my new job and all of a sudden, I unpack "not good enough," so now on your first day on the post, you hear the manager saying, "I wanted to go with the other client, but they weren't available, but I chose you because you were our number two." You've heard that they wanted someone else, but that came into your reality from what you had in that bag of not being good enough from the start. Now, you begin to have an attitude. You start to work harder. You're trying to prove your existence for being there without ever feeling that you belong there. You're moving so fast that you're making mistakes. You're doing things trying to stay relevant to the point you're not doing anything right. Before you know it, there are problems on the job, problems with your meeting deadlines, questions that you had inside of your head because, from the moment you overheard the conversation, you'd already lost the job. You put yourself twenty or thirty years in a position where you never felt like you were good enough.

Now, think about the very religious institution itself— your church or wherever you go. You go there looking for acceptance, but you begin to unpack the same baggage. You start to form friends in the church and begin to form hate. Beginning to form groups, and before you know it, there are arguments and discussions because they want this choir member over you. They prefer their voice over yours. They like this over that and now, every time you turn around, this baggage comes with you and begins to unpack. I want to ask you a question: Who are you when you've lost yourself? Who are you when you're defined by what's in the bag and you're trying to take the bag to people and say, "Please accept me. Please, am I good enough for you?" But the bag is inauthentic, and it becomes, I tried over and over and over again until finally, I found someone who would just settle with the baggage-- and you lived your life unhappily ever after.

2

THE GIFT THAT WE BURIED

It is funny how in life, we spend our time observing others. Each day, we watch new people who come into our atmospheres and ease their way into our realities. We find that some make us happy, some make us laugh, some make us angry. They give us all different types of emotions. Have you ever noticed that it is often easier to observe others than to see yourself? Take a moment and come outside of your body. What you're going to do is simply look down and observe yourself. There are some patterns that you repeat. There are some things in relationships that you do over and over —the same thing— looking for a different reaction from people. Most people live life in a flow by just taking whatever life throws at them, but they never manage to take control of their lives because they don't know how. The first thing I want you to do when observing yourself is to watch your life. Watch what you do from the outside, and not so much from the inside. Watch how you interact with the people in your world. Are you defending attitudes? Are you in connection with people until things go wrong? Do you find yourself blaming others? While observing yourself, you'll see things that you don't like, but what I want you to do is focus on the things you do like and the undeniable gifts you have.

Often, before a child is named in some cultures, the elders observe the child to see what gift they possess. Then, the child is called according to the gift. For example, if the child shows the ability to work with his or her hands and put things together, they would be named accordingly. If the child demonstrates the ability to think or problem solve, the name given would reflect this. The point is that whatever they name the child, each time they call that child's name, they are always calling and reminding them of their gift.

Now, most people will start to live from the point of trauma. When you ask them to go back into their past, they get choked up or emotional. They have all of these different reactions from being asked a question about their history.

Society has groomed us to whenever we go to the past; there's a troubling part from where we start and where we continue. Imagine only going back to the trouble: the molestation, the abuse. Imagine only going back to that point every time and starting your life from that. You will see that when you do this—when you live life from the trauma, you will always seem to connect with people who remind you of the wound. What I want you to think about is not the trauma you've endured, but the gift you came here with.

Every one of us has an undeniable gift. When you observe yourself, you will begin to see that you demonstrate a pattern of abilities everywhere you go. Let's see the real story behind the gift. This world works by connection— by one person helping ignite another. One person's contribution is added to another person's, and you begin to create things to move forward. I don't want you to think about how you're stuck or how many people are stuck; I want you to think of the simple purpose of why you're here. Before you come through the womb and the moment you exit the womb, you will demonstrate a gift. Think of this as if you're in a classroom taking an exam. Before the test, the teacher says, "Hey, here's a curve. I'm going to give you fifteen points before we start the exam." You received credit before you took the test. I want you to think about this with your gift. It is not something you just developed. It was given to you. If you believe that you are alone in this universe, then my friend, you are sadly mistaken.

A gift understands you before you know yourself, and when it comes to you, it becomes your atmosphere. Now I want you to stop right there and think about that learning curve, this gift, this atmosphere.

QUESTION:

How do others describe the energy they feel when you enter a room? This is your atmosphere.

You may write these words down as they say them. The point is to see what people say about you when you enter a room. How do you make them feel? Please take the time to ask two or three people this question. You're going to find out when you begin to look and talk to people; they're going to say the same thing. For example, "You make me feel uplifted. You make me feel happy. You make me feel encouraged." They will go on and on about your atmosphere even before you open your mouth. Your gift came into the room before you.

Now think about this: no matter where you go, no matter how old you are, that gift— not the trauma— follows you. However, if you don't know yourself, you will not know your gift. You will find yourself running into people who take advantage or control of your talents. Think about it. It's undeniable; we all have a gift. Many people will say that they don't know what theirs is, but it is unquestionable. When you write down your capabilities, you're going to begin to see yourself in a different light— "Something gave me this gift, and all I have to do is tie into it throughout my life, and it will produce."

TASK:

Take a moment to write down your gifts; the unique capabilities or talents you possess.

You're born into a destiny. You're born into a purpose, and you were not put here alone. The same thing that gave you the gift is the same thing that will create a way for you to use it. Many people drift away from their gifts and become the exact opposite. Take the time to find out everything that is in your atmosphere. You're going to have this gift that, when used correctly, will change, create, and help everyone who comes into your reality, but the first person you must help with this power is yourself.

If you look at people, every one of them carries a gift. Some aren't using theirs. They may be employed by others who are taking advantage of it. The gift is your business. It goes into everything you touch. Some people allow others to manage their skills; however, your gift belongs to you. It was created to bring you into the presence of great people. It is designed to get you into the company of kings. Most importantly, it is used to tie you into purpose and create connections throughout the universe. Think about how gifted you are. Many will think about how traumatized they were, but to know yourself, you have to see this learning curve that you have been given. You have to become a perfectionist concerning yourself. When you're observing yourself, observe how you made people happy, see how you were a peacemaker, and couldn't rest until the mission was accomplished.

TASK:

Write down your observations concerning yourself.

Imagine walking into a room and knowing your atmosphere — knowing that you bring encouragement, are uplifting, healing. Some mess up when they try to become something other than their atmosphere. After you observe yourself and find out what manner of person you are, you will know what you carry in your atmosphere. For example, when you enter a room and deliverance occurs, and every time you open your mouth, your vision begins to help people get delivered from their setbacks. So, you open your mouth until people are uplifted and set free. You are then using your environment, your atmosphere, your gift to help make people better, and that, my friend, is a beautiful thing. When I use my gift, and you use yours, we will find ourselves in a place of connection like never before.

3

PUTTING ON A COSTUME

As I have stated, we all have a gift. No one can bypass that. You're born into this strange, mysterious world. Before we go any further, we're going to talk about the universal law of polarity. In getting a good understanding of polarity, it says that everything exists on another plane. There cannot be good without evil, joy without pain; success cannot exist without failure. Everything is connected to the direct struggle from whence it came. This is going to become very important as you begin to discover who you are.

Let's imagine that somewhere out there, there's a positive and negative side of the universe. The positive side is your atmosphere. It is the things that you are born with; your joyfulness, your uplifting vibes, your ability to cause deliverance. These are the positive sides of the atmosphere. There's also a negative side to the universe. The negative side sees your gift before you can see it yourself, such is life. Most people can see your gift and know how to either shut it down or enhance it as life goes on, but the negative side sees the gift, sees the potential, and begins to use the law of polarity. It goes on to say this: if I can create the perfect storm— the perfect day in their life by understanding who they are to offset those gifts, I can embed it in their subconscious mind, that they become the opposite of what their gifts are. I want you to think about the day in your life that things began to change. Now, here's where the trauma begins to come in. We've observed ourselves. We saw our gifts.

QUESTION:

If your gifts had never been challenged,
who would you be today?

That means looking at yourself with all of these abilities. If you would just see yourself from the gifts, what would you have turned out to be this day? What type of kid were you? How did you demonstrate these gifts? Were you a leader?

Did you run the community club? Did you organize the gang? Were you a follower of the group? Did we move by your ideas while being a kid? Did you choose what we were going to play? I want you to observe that. If left unchecked, you would have been something remarkable or more impressive than what you already are.

Because the negative side of the universe comes in and has known you before you knew yourself, it needed to create a reality. It needed to create something that you would see. It would change your whole perception about life before you got to know who you were. Think about it, something messed up your life, and it knew who you were before you had the power to see who you were yourself. So, now you're a kid, and you're walking around and playing unstoppably. You have laughter. You have joy. You have not been afraid of anything or anyone. When you set your mind to do something, you do it without fear. Then, one day as you walked closer to the house, you begin to hear an argument. Maybe there was a punch thrown, or maybe your situation was something else. There was abuse. There was molestation. There was something that began to happen that caused you to no longer walk in the gifts but in a cruel reality of what this life could be. Now, it's in these moments when no one tells you what to think or how to respond that you begin to foster a belief system. You begin to create a creed, a statement, a truth — and it stands still and starts to embed into your spirit.

"I'll never love because love hurts."

"I'll never open up."

"I will not communicate."

Whatever it was, it formed your belief system. This moment was the beginning of something else taking control of your life that understood you better than you understood yourself.

Now, let's go back to that room and sit there. This thing has just happened to you, and you've formed these beliefs: I'm not worthy, no one's going to hear me, no one understands me. Now, this is a critical time because you're forming the beliefs. You're around seven, eight, or twelve years old, shaping the ideas that will set a pattern throughout the rest of your life.

You are so powerful, but you don't know how to use your power. Whenever you make these statements, it doesn't matter how much personal development you do; you cannot override the beliefs that you've established in your spirit. There's a process to get to this, and we'll talk about that later on. Right now, I want you to think about the day that altered your life. I know that psychology teaches you to hold on to that moment. I know you're told that who you are between those years is who you're going to be, but that is not what this transformation is all about. This is about creating change because people need change, and they don't need systems, and they don't need diagnoses. The power is within you to change. Everything you need is within you.

At this moment, we know you've changed. We know that the smile has disappeared, and you have begun to become another person. There's a moment when you feel as if people have turned their backs on you. There's a moment when you feel as if people don't love you. There is a moment when you begin to turn your back on the child within you, holding the gift. When you turn on that child carrying the gifts, you begin to put on a costume and behavior patterns form. You put on an entire costume, not just a face mask, and it is the first step to becoming inauthentic. You begin to think, "Now, I have to compete to feel like I'm good enough." Now, you start to form a question based on the hurt you've experienced. Every one of us goes through life trying to find answers. These are the years when the questions are forming. I want you to think about what questions you have. Every relationship you get into, you question, "Am I good enough? Am I smart enough?" You begin to go into these concerns because someone made you feel like you were not heard, that you were not intelligent, that you were not worthy— so you began to go throughout life asking a question, "Am I now what I knew that I was when I came into this world?" You're no longer sure of yourself and the precious gifts you have; you become the exact opposite.

TASK:

Write down the words that describe your atmosphere.

Then, write down the opposite of those words.

This will explain where you are today. When you were a child, being listened to was a gift; now, you're feeling ignored. You possessed the gift of being a leader. Now, you find yourself being a follower with someone making you feel like you can't even think for yourself. There is an opposite that the negative side of the universe understood. It knew that one day, one perception— if it took control of the most influential thing that you have, your beliefs, and made you believe against yourself, it could control everywhere you go in life and every outcome. Look at the list. Look at how accurate it is. Look at how you're drawing people in your life who make you feel like the opposite of who you truly are. Polarity says that the truth is inside of you. The truth is always there. You go on a journey at this time. You put on this costume, and start a trip away from your reality. This costume doesn't feel right. This costume is negotiating life. It is figuring life out, trying to get acceptance from those who rejected you. You never think about how you brought in "not being good enough" or turning your back on the little kid who was holding the gift.

Now, you've put on a costume and live a life away from your gifts. The gifts are steadily trailing along. They're still entering rooms with you. Now, everyone else can see them, but they've gone away from you where you can no longer see them. You've put on a costume, my friend, and you're living life in it even today. But, that costume is not your truth. You've put on something that isn't you, and now it sets the stage everywhere you go for an inauthentic life.

4

COLLECTING BAGGAGE

Here it is: for the first time in your life, you made a statement in your subconscious. You made a declaration. For the first time, you were living life. You were having fun— enjoying the ride. Before we go any further, you need to identify your truths. Your truth may not be real, but it's something that you've said to protect yourself or form a new relationship with yourself that allows you to navigate this world. It's based on an experience or someone else's opinion. When you begin to put on this costume, it takes on a mind of its own. Now you go through life not feeling good enough, not feeling worthy, not feeling accepted. When you go through life wearing this costume, you begin to draw people into your reality. When these people come into your reality, they are responding to the costume, and before long, you may start to read this and realize that everything in your life may be a result of the costume. A belief that you formed that wasn't even real— and everything in your life that you're facing could be untrue.

One begins to collect baggage. One begins to collect teachers over and over again. Have you ever been in a relationship with someone—got out of the relationship and into a new one with someone else, and they look different but act the same way and do the same things? You, my friend, must learn from these teachers that you are manifesting. Other than that, it would be an endless pile of baggage that we begin to look through for different experiences, but deep down inside—carrying the same beliefs. You cannot manifest the opposite of what you believe at your core, but you will continue to draw repeat teachers. How does that look? There was an argument that you overheard or an experience that you had with a parent where they made you feel like you weren't good enough, but when you left the house, no one came behind you and said, "We had a disagreement. We didn't mean any harm. We said some things that we didn't mean." No damage control was done. During these times, when you go to your room, you begin to develop that belief "They said this to me because I'm not good enough, and if a parent said it, it must be true." Now, you go outside, and the neighborhood kids are picking people to be on the team. They choose everyone except you. Here's the same thing being repeated—I'm not good enough. I'm not acceptable. Now, it moves on to your friends. They choose everyone else for relationships and dating, except you. You have to go home and adjust to it. You've got the belief. Now you have to put on the adjustment. Now, you've become this overbearing person who begins to put their body out there before their mind. You begin to form all of these beliefs about yourself. Now you have to behave like someone you're not.

Imagine having the truth in you and not knowing it. Imagine living a life from the basis of trying to be what you already are— trying to become the truth that's already in you. Now, you're going on a journey farther and farther away from it. Everything in your life becomes one bad experience after the next. You get in a relationship, give up your body, and when it's all said and done, they begin to make you feel the same. They say things linked to what your father said. They do things related to what your mother said. You see results before you know it, but I want to inform you that the costume is getting the results. This baggage begins to follow you. Now, you've altered your personality. You've become what you think people want from you. You become overbearing and try to do any and everything just to be accepted. You've gone on a long journey away from yourself. If you look at the behavior patterns you have now, is it your correct behavior pattern, or is it a response to what someone said? What they said made you feel like you weren't being heard, now you go on and try to explain yourself to people. You find yourself talking too much. You find yourself over-communicating. You find yourself feeling that in all that you do, still, no one is listening to you. You start a behavior pattern. How many different costumes are you wearing? How many different levels are there to you— and none of these levels represent who you truly are?

The average person is putting on a facade. They're carrying baggage and trying to make life work from the baggage. It is almost safe to say that nothing you see is real, but everyone you look at is an adjustment. An adjustment that is sitting on top of a truth they have grown far from. When you start to talk to them about certain things, they begin to cry. They begin to go to psychologists seeking help, but what's happening is they all have a suit on, a costume that's bringing the same baggage to them over and over again. It is a manifestation. Whatever you thought when you sat in that room in hurt, whatever you believed about yourself when you heard that argument becomes the most powerful thing in the universe, and it is consistent with the results that it's creating in your life. Think about life. You're still wearing a costume. You're in a relationship right now with someone in costume. The real you has yet to be seen. This baggage becomes hurtful. It sets the stage for abuse. It sets the stage for you to take a question out there, and for everyone to answer your question the same way. They're answering this question because you don't know your truth. What is it you're seeking? What is it you're trying to find where it seems like life is just sustaining you? Where everything is always working out at the last minute— always at 11:59, and you're happy because it came through, then you go through the same cycle again.

Spirit will maintain you, but it will not let you walk into a purpose until you walk in there the right way. You'll get to the place where you really understand the truth. You will be glad that you didn't get what you wanted when you wanted it. The minute something works out for an inauthentic person, a person who shows up with baggage, the baggage will forever be there. Life sometimes cannot work out with this baggage. You have to identify what you're carrying right now that are just bags of untruths about yourself. When we get through this, you'll begin to see life in an entirely different light. You'll start to see life on a platform. That's never happened before, but you must identify the baggage you're carrying, the personality you're carrying, the things you're carrying that are an adaptation to what someone said —mainly you inside your head. When you said, "I'm not good enough," you began putting on a facade that "I am good enough!" When you said, "I'm not worthy," you started to put on a play to pretend as if you're worthy. Sometimes the people who speak the loudest are hurting the most on the inside. Sometimes, people trying to prove something the most are those who don't believe in themselves or their abilities. What is your baggage? Financial baggage? Where you believe you're only worth a certain amount, so the manifestations that are showing up in your life do not suggest or complement the gift that is inside you. You're walking around with less. You're walking around with baggage that is continuously hurting you over and over again.

5

COUNTERFEIT

Why does it seem like so many of us are just getting along? We find ourselves living from paycheck to paycheck, only having enough to work harder the next month. We don't understand why, but it seems like as much as we try to get out, we can only manifest just enough to make it to the next pay period. What if these results weren't really your results? What if these results that you were getting were just something to maintain you, but not your truth? Keeping you alive; Keeping you functioning, because it has to obey a process. There are some things in life when you think about it, you will be glad you didn't experience it. What if life wanted you to walk in your truth before it can open up the door? First, before any of that can happen, you have to see the costume you're wearing.

Let's think about this thing. Most of our manifestation begins early in life between seven and twelve years old. In those years, we begin to form subconscious beliefs that will one day shape our experiences and reality. Now, imagine something that you saw as a kid, and as we said earlier, this is something that no one has taken the time to explain to you and has caused you to form beliefs. Let's go back inside the house. Perhaps you thought it was your fault that your father or mother left, so you began to blame yourself. You began to think, "Had I been a better child, my parent wouldn't have left home" and you sit with that. What you sit with becomes the most powerful thing in the universe. Later on, you will learn the art of seed planting, little suggestions with significant effects. You sit with an idea, and you say, "My father left because of me. I'm not good enough." Then, you put that "I'm not good enough" barrier around your life. When you begin to believe that barrier, you move to the next part of your life carrying it. Maybe you go to school, and the team captains choose everyone, except you. You find yourself being laughed at, pushed aside, judged. You started a belief, and life begins to form to what you believe.

Let's go a little bit further in life. Let's say now you put on a behavioral pattern because of this. You start to put on a behavioral practice that you're going to be more forward. You're going to be the initiator because you don't want to deal with rejection. You're going to put yourself out there, lowering your character and lowering your standards. You're in a relationship where someone makes you feel you're not good enough. You're working a job where you feel not good enough. You develop a self-sabotaging behavior. The same behavior you displayed to get attention is the very behavior that knocks attention away from you. Now, all of your life—think about it— your mate never saw your value, your job never saw your worth, your friends never saw your value. Everything is holding reliable based on the belief system that you created. My friend, I ask you a question: How could you get anything more than just sustainability when you're showing up in a person that is not the truth? Imagine something so small, a seed, a perception that you saw as minute that became something significant. I ask you now to examine your life. How many belief systems have you formed that are still controlling you?

To be honest, if you think about it, you could be so deep into that manifestation that you're not present today. The world is getting a version of you, it's getting an untruth of you, and you're taking that untruth and trying to make reality work for you. This costume that we all wear produces a fake life; The life of a person who believes that they're not good enough based on a decision that they made as a child. This makes the child the most vital thing in the universe. It is said in scripture that a child shall lead them and suffer not a child to come unto me for such is the kingdom of God (Isaiah 11:6, Matthew 19:14). A little child is the most powerful thing in the universe because most adults are walking around with decisions that they made in their youth. That step you made so young could have an enormous effect, but I need you to understand that this manifestation, although it may not be what you wanted in life, proves that manifestation is real. Some people say, "Well, why doesn't the law of attraction work for me?" The law of attraction is working for your costume because you are manifesting what you believe in your subconscious that you're not good enough. Everything that you bring into your life, you have the baggage to unpack for it. Every place that you go, you start unpacking "not good enough." I could give you a million dollars right now, and you will begin to have a negative manifestation because that goes against your truth. You believe that riches are for good enough people, and because you don't feel good enough, you will begin to spend this money or have things happen in your life that will take this money away because it goes against your programming. That's right, programming.

Programming is when you stack the subconscious mind with enough evidence that it begins to take hold of that belief. If you sit there every day saying, "I'm not good enough," the subconscious mind will pick it up, and the ego forms. You will have behavior patterns that will prove that you're not good enough. Having said that, what costume are you wearing right now? What belief system are you honoring? What understanding are you still holding on to ever since childhood? Remember, the trick is for you to become the opposite of your atmosphere. If that negative side of the universe can trick you out of your authority, it can control you everywhere you go. Some people say it's the devil. I say it's not the devil. It's what we created. It is us responding to a stimulus, responding to an ideology that was planted. "I'm not good enough" —we don't need a devil to speak into our ear. If we have the right belief about ourselves or say the wrong idea about ourselves, we will manifest the results accordingly. When you think about your costume, you'll get to a place in life where you're glad that things didn't work out. If it would've worked out while you're wearing that costume, you would have forever believed that you weren't good enough. Anything that comes into your life that is sustainable could cause you to go throughout life believing a lie, and you would pass that lie along to your children. Your costume controls your finances. It manages your love life. It maintains your friendships. It controls everything, but it is doing just what it's supposed to do. When you stack it with belief, the belief will manifest.

Everyone you see may be wearing some type of costume. Look at this person. They're engaging in all kinds of sexual activity with people trying to find their value under that sex. They're looking for someone who makes them feel worthy because someone took away their worth. When you begin to see life like this, you will see everyone in the costumes they're wearing, and by looking at the outfit, you can be pretty sure of the results they're bringing in their life right now. These costumes are uncomfortable. These costumes are full of heartache, but one thing about it, it teaches you that manifestation is consistent and constant. When you look at your life, let this be a testimony that if you manifest something bad without trying, you can manifest that which is really for you when you have knowledge of self. Imagine what that day would look like when you know your truth because it is written that the truth shall set you free. When you find yourself, you will begin to see all the different shifts. Good things will start to happen in your life, but first, I need you to identify every area you are wearing a costume. Costumes are protected by ego. Costumes are protected by self-sabotaging behaviors.

QUESTION:

What areas in your life are you wearing a costume?

6

LIVING A SETTLED LIFE

Everything we put our finger on, we leave our signature. Whatever bags you bring, whatever masks you wear, everything from that point on bears your mark. Think about life and think about your wedding day when you learned to put that mask on or that entire costume that bears rejection, feelings of not being good enough, and unworthiness. It finds its way into the relationship, and sometimes it makes its way to the alter. Now, when you're not worthy because of those manifestations in the back of your head, you draw in someone who makes you feel that way. I want to challenge that: is it that you thought that, you manifested it, or is it that you brought this person into your reality based off of your baggage? Everywhere you go, you begin to control your outcomes. This lesson will be powerful because it will teach you that you are the results you get in life and that if you can change you, you can change everything that comes into your life. Now, by the time you say your wedding agreements, the signs have already manifested. You have little arguments here and there. Then, bigger fights that get you to that wedding day and what happens is "I'm not good enough" is staring in the face of "I'll make you feel not good enough." Then, "unworthy" is gazing in the face of "I'm going to show you that you have no worth." You get married and go on about your life. The arguments begin to manifest even more because marriage would prove that you have worth so that when you deem yourself unworthy, the trials and tribulations begin.

When you get in that marriage, there is this thing called sabotage. Sabotage is the behavior that you take on based on that belief in the back of your head. For example, when I don't feel good enough, I begin to be overly talkative — trying to be seen. When I don't feel worthy, I begin to try to find my worth in any and everything. You see, for every limiting belief, there's sabotage. When sabotage comes into the relationship, the cold hard fact is that many people get married without ever knowing who they married. When two masks marry each other, the truth is buried. Older folks would say, "Well, when trials come, that's nothing but the devil trying you," but I'm here to tell you that the devil does not have to try or attack any seed he has planted. When you pick up the limiting belief, you also bring the manifestation with you. The power given to you to subdue this earth now becomes the same power used to destroy everything you put your hands on.

We will look at this relationship and the things that begin to happen. You're walking and talking, and all of a sudden, you take offense to something that was said. That offense goes toward the unworthiness that lies within you. You brush it off. It happens again, then you argue. When you're discussing the issue, the argument must validate your unworthiness, so you go ahead and find a temporary worth, but that is not what you're programmed to receive. So, again, the arguments happen over and over again, and it brings you back to feeling unworthy. Now, you say it's their fault that you feel this way. It's their fault that you feel less than your worth, but did you not, in fact, bring unworthiness into the game? When you brought unworthiness, you were already a manifesting machine. So, from your wedding vows until the day of the divorce, you worked toward the "I'm not good enough." Wouldn't it be amazing to find out that your marriage never had a chance? Wouldn't it be amazing to find out that what you thought was love was no more than a grand show of self-sabotage?

I want you to think about your relationship right now. You have battle lines drawn. You know what to do and what not to do. You know what's offensive and what's inoffensive. Somewhere along the second year, you begin to go up for either divorce or the great settlement. When you start to settle, there are two people with battle lines drawn who don't really know each other. You have a decision to make. Do you stay in or do you get out? In talking to them and catching them at the point of divorce, most people found out that their spouse never knew them and was on their way out of the door from the beginning. How is someone supposed to know you when you don't even know yourself? All you're doing is creating the same scenarios. When you get out of that settlement, you go into the next relationship with a more in-depth bid to reach the point of your limiting beliefs. Therefore, everywhere you go, the limiting beliefs are manifesting the same things over and over again. I always tell a person —if you can see how you manifested the bad, then the good should be no problem. When you settle, keep in mind that everything that you put your finger on bears your signature.

Now, it goes into your job. You go onto the job, "not good enough." You bring "not worthy," but you, my friend, are a walking manifestation that will not be satisfied until you prove that truth to yourself. So, you go on the job and get asked to do something outside of your comfort zone, and immediately, you begin to take offense, "Why are they picking on me? Is it because I don't have my degree? Is it because I don't have as much training as everyone else?" We bring that manifestation into the place with an attitude to match. So, when you look at it, no matter what they do, you're going to take offense to it because you brought this —your signature. You began to unpack these things when they hired you for the job. From the moment you shook hands, you'd already handed in your resignation. Everything becomes offensive, and now we see the sabotage. When I don't feel good enough on the job, I constantly try to prove myself. I'm consistently going above and beyond. I'm continually trying to find worth in the words "good job," and I'm asking people "Didn't I do a good job? Was it enough? How did you like it?" Now we're searching after that worth. It becomes overbearing for your coworkers, and because you're working to prove something instead of working toward a purpose, you're slowly leading yourself toward the same manifestation. Now, you're staying on the job until nine or ten at night while your family is lacking. At nine or ten o'clock at night, you find yourself doing busy work. Nine or ten o'clock at night when you should be home, satisfied with what you've done for the day, you never feel like it's enough. So, you show up early, "Didn't I do this? Didn't I do that?" When the manager finally begins to see it, they see it as a hard worker who lacks confidence because they do not believe in themself. The next thing you know, you begin to get side eyes from coworkers. You begin to have a name around the office, and all the time, you never started your job, you started trying to prove your worth.

Now, you look at other factors —other things that you bring into the workplace. It's you against the world. No one cares for you. Nobody likes you. So, on the job, you become problematic. You search out people, and everything that they say offends you. Before you know it, you lose your fire, you have an attitude, and you begin to settle. This settlement follows you to the relationship with yourself. The same things that happened in the marriage, the same things that happened on the job, all stem from you. When you're unworthy, your outfit shows it; your character shows it, you won't take the chances that you would typically take, fearful of the very promise land that you want so badly. Imagine wanting something so badly; every day you want it, but the very thing that you want, you drive away. Those feelings of being unworthy cause you to wave your hands and say, "Here I am, here I am!" so loudly, you run everyone away from you. You will not rest until you settle and manifest your truth. I ask you right now, what is your truth in your relationships with others? What is your truth on your job? What is your truth with your relationship with yourself? You're saying, "No one takes me seriously," but I ask you the question: Do you take yourself seriously? "No one likes me." I ask you the question: Do you like yourself? You're going to find out that self is the breeding ground for everything that goes on.

This world will mirror how you treat yourself. Whatever you utter inside of your head will become your reality. You have to understand that even from birth, there's a fight. A fight to get you to settle. A fight to get you to give up on your gift. Ever since you came onto this earth, there was a fight to control your mind because if something can control your mind, it can control your reality. Have you settled? Have you settled with you in one room and your husband sleeping in another? Have you settled because all you gave him was "unworthy"? All you gave her was "not good enough." I invite you to go into the bedroom. I invite you to take your mask off, and I advise you to equip yourself with the tools that you need so that your truth can finally begin to live. I know you settled. I know that right now, while you're reading this, the happenings that you want aren't there. It is elusive to you, but that blessing cannot find you until you find yourself.

7

THE SEEDS YOU MAKE

Again I say, everything you put your finger on leaves your signature. We looked at the marriage. We looked at the relationship with self. We looked at your employment. Now, what we're going to do is look at what's closest to you, your seed. Whatever business you leave unfinished, your child will have to continue to handle. Either they will make it, or it won't allow them to get any farther than you got in their day in time. Think about conception; when not good enough, and other energies come together, they begin to create a seed. The very act of creating that seed is searching for worth. The very act of that seed is "not good enough" or feeling unworthy. From the time that seed is in the womb, it's listening and hearing this struggle. Its internal dialect is in your subconscious mind, and when this child is born, he or she is already born into your bloodline struggle. Remember, this didn't start with you. It started with your parents. It began before them and made it all the way up through you. Mom never reached her goals. You're struggling to find your path, and now you bring the baby into this world with "I'm not good enough." So, from the time they begin to walk, they're walking with this subconscious energy, and one day, it becomes a reality. The same cycle begins to start all over again. The seed —the very thing that you have that's a representative of your bloodline.

Let's talk bloodline for a minute. A bloodline is something that will try to purge itself until truth comes, and it may take two hundred to two thousand years for this truth to be birthed. We call them black sheep. Black sheep are those who are born to bring about change. Oftentimes they find themselves rejected, not invited to the party. They don't feel like they fit in anywhere. These black sheep are born with the issues that you had times ten. Those issues form the same way they started with you. They begin to form when they go into the schoolyard and meet that one bully, that one kid who will open up the door for a manifestation. Now, the coach is choosing the basketball team, and they don't pick him. It stands out, and the most lonely, coldest feeling comes upon him, "They chose everyone else but me." At this time, he begins to bear your stripes. He won't talk to you about it. It becomes the most impersonal thing. The next day, he goes back to school, and his peers say, "Well, we're putting this group together," and they overlook him. They ignore him looking to everyone else. Again, he walks home with the same thing, the unworthiness. Now your seed is bearing your mark, and you cannot recognize it because you have yet to deal with the issue yourself. Now there's a pullback. The very thing that he's gifted to do. The very atmosphere that he's been blessed to share is on hold.

Let's talk about the atmosphere. This child comes into the world, bearing the same gifts as you. The opposite of unworthy is worthy. The opposite of not good enough is good enough. So even before this child gets started walking, he has an atmosphere to win. This atmosphere that he has is the same that you had. Somebody's got to win. So, now this child walks in and something happens one day. This day brings the exact opposite of what he feels about himself. He becomes a backward manifestation; the same as you. Now, he's going to have to go on a journey to find his true gifts. Imagine trying to find yourself without a roadmap. Imagine trying to find yourself, and you have no one to show you how you're messing up. One thing that happens is we begin to see ourselves in our children, and then we bump heads and don't get along because there's too much of what happened in you happening in them. So, what does your seed represent right now? Take a moment to find out what those limiting beliefs are that you have. Take time and talk to your children about those same limiting beliefs. If you want to have a conversation that will bond you with your child, have the conversation around unworthiness, but first, before you can carry a message, you have to be the message. Seeds do not respond to what we tell them; they react to what we live in our subconscious mind. Have you ever seen a child who wouldn't stop crying? Have you ever noticed a child who had anxiety? That child is bearing what you wouldn't express. That child is exhibiting characteristics of what you wouldn't release. What you don't remove is born in them. You must find yourself and develop a conversation with that child. Everything we put our finger on we recreate. Everywhere we go, we leave our signature.

It is one thing to leave unpacked baggage on the job —but it's another thing to leave it for a generation, allowing it to exist two to three hundred years after you're born. Back in the day, there were signet rings and family crests. These were given to the children. They were shown to the kids so that once they found out who they were, they could look at the crest and see where they came from whenever they got discouraged. Imagine our children today who can't even see where they came from, and most of the time, when shown where they came from, they came from a place with a lot of hurt and pain. Look at what your father did to me. Look at what my mother did to me, but we never look at the manifestation that we're carrying in that bag everywhere we go. The same way that you went through life, you pass it along to your kids. If you want to fix anything, you can never point the finger at the next person. The finger must come toward you. You are the key. When your ego is in control, it blows up everyone else, "Look at what they did to me." But when the true spirit takes over, it shows you yourself first. When it shows you yourself, it's not showing you to punish you; it's showing you to get rid of the things on the inside that are holding you back.

8

MASK OFF

We've looked at how this baggage is passed along to our seed. Now, let's look at what it has caused to happen in our relationships and on the job. You might ask yourself: How is it that we begin to heal what is broken or if it can even be healed at all? Remember, psychology would suggest that the way you are by a certain age is the way you shall be, but I want to interject something new. In order to heal what is, you must go back to what was. So many people try the equivalent of "stop smoking, stop doing drugs" —just stop, but there is no stopping without going to the pathway that caused it in the first place. So much of our history, our structure is built around psychology, around trauma, but for one minute, I want you to do something that very few people will ask you to do. Think back before anything went wrong, before any abuse, before any downing of yourself, go back to the beginning because that is where the truth lies. Let me remind you that the child is the most vital thing in the universe. The child? Why do you say that? The child comes into the earth bearing the gift and exhibits this gift straight out of the womb. No one has to tell this child what to do. One day they pick up blocks and begin to build an entire neighborhood. One day they make tents, and the next, they climb trees. The very things that you did in play were designed for you to do in reality.

The way that this world works is that everyone comes in with a gift. Very few people find their way to using that gift, but it is designed to cause connection. I want you to think about it. Have you ever used your gift? Have you ever released that which was in you, or do you feel so unworthy you cannot use that gift? Once a child undergoes trauma, the trauma begins to control the manifestation. The last time they saw their true gift was the day before the "it" happened in their life. Now, with that gift, God grants everyone an atmosphere. Keep in mind that your atmosphere is something that you do and don't even know it. Earlier, you had to ask three people the question, "When I enter a room without opening up my mouth, how do I make you feel?" You found that most people began to utter your atmosphere with,"Well, you make me feel secure," but you feel insecure. They told you, "You make me feel trusted," but you feel untrusted. They will tell you what is in your atmosphere. This atmosphere gave you a head start, and it will always announce the gift. So, even before you open your mouth, you have favor.

Now, let's go beyond that to what we were saying earlier about looking at our past. Let's pull back a minute, and if you've ever watched *A Christmas Carol* and remember the ghost of Christmas past, this is how you should look back. For a minute, let's go back to what you were doing as a little child? You may find yourself a busy body all over the place, being creative, drawing, singing, laughing. No one taught you how to do these things, but this is what you find yourself doing. Before any trauma started, you were a visionary. Before any trauma started, you were creative, and you could organize. Before anything started, you had the gift to uplift, the gift to bring smiles, the gift to give direction, and the list goes on. Why is it that the last time you saw your gift was during your childhood? Before we can begin unmasking, we have to know what truth we're about to face.

There is an old saying that the truth shall set you free. The only thing that can go beyond science, the only thing that can go beyond psychology, my friend, is the truth. When you go back and look at the truth about your life, the unmasking begins. Now you begin to see something. It becomes almost an equation, almost ancient science, and when you look at your gift, you'll find out that the day the "it" happened directly challenged your gift. It is polarity.

Polarity in the universe is everything. You cannot have sadness without happiness. You cannot have joy without having pain. When your gift shows up, the negative portion of the universe wants the polarity of that gift. Imagine walking around in this world the very opposite of who you're supposed to be. In some cases, it may even be comical that the strongest people in the world won't even stand up because they feel like they're the weakest. Whatever your atmosphere is, there you are. No matter how far you try to run away from your pain, there you are, and you've got to learn to look toward the atmosphere when you doubt yourself. You have to learn to look toward the atmosphere when you feel like you're unworthy. Know thyself is what we say. The most ancient form of communication is knowing thyself, which is the beginning of knowing your authentic self. You weren't created to be powerless. You were created to be a part of this universe to cause connection.

Many of us are sleeping on our gifts because we're walking around backward. We're walking around accepting less than who we were created to be. Now that you know He created us to do something, you say, "Well, I don't want to be like that because it's not humble." I want to tell you this: if you were created to be a light, it is a sin to go back in front of God being less than who He created you to be. So, whatever He set forth for you, this is the process of starting to embrace all of it, unapologetically, to the point where you owe no excuses for what He created. First, we must understand and embrace what it is that He created.

Now, as you educate yourself, we call upon the ghost of Christmas future. We fast forward life and the same little kid without the trauma —what would that kid be doing with that gift on this day? By the time this is over, you may find out that you're sitting on a job that you were always overqualified for from day one. You may find out that you were in a relationship that you deserved more from since day one. When the future begins to roll, and your gift begins to speak into the universe, you will see yourself. When you see this, get ready to embrace it. You are whatever you think yourself to be. That polarity will find you, and we'll talk about polarity more, but right now, I need you to get real familiar with the atmosphere and the gift. You see yourself in the future. The same little kid who was playing with blocks is now an architect. The same little kid building tents is now creating homes for the homeless; structure for those who don't have it. That same person who was organizing the toys begins to organize people's lives. You may be working a job and supposed to be in a whole different field, a whole different reality, but the day you wake up, everything begins to erase. So, you must know your truth because, again, I say, the truth shall set you free.

You've been a walking gift. The power comes in when you sit with the truth. The coaches didn't pick you to be on the football team, and you went home and sat with it. You sat with it until you began to be down on yourself, "Well, they didn't choose me because I'm too little. They didn't choose me because I'm not good enough" —and you sat with that. What you sat in became so powerful that you're still getting its results until this day. The greatest power in this universe is the ability to sit with a thought and chew on it. You chewed on something and got divorced because of it. You chewed on something, and all of the family is torn because of it. Now

I say if you can sit on that and bring these manifestations in your life, isn't it about time to sit on the truth? When you sit on the truth, it begins to unravel. Imagine sitting with the knowledge that you're "greater than," knowing that it came from a higher power than you. Imagine sitting on the truth and letting it begin to take over your life.

You've been taught to do your "I Am" affirmations, but why quote an "I Am" based on something you're not connected to? The "I Am's" should be developed by the atmosphere. They should be based on the gift. Spend time every day speaking into that gift that is called your life. When you begin to lather and stand in that gift, the mask begins to fall off.

9

THIS LIGHT OF MINE

The song says, "This little light of mine, I'm gonna let it shine." Now, as you're sitting there, your power begins to come. You begin to learn the truth; that ever since you were born, there was an attack on your gift, an attack to break harmony. That attack to make your light not show up in this world. Each of us will find out that there's not one of us who was born without a light. When you begin to see your gift, that is the beginning of everything. When you start to see it, you will understand why the universe's negative side began to attack you so severely. Your gift is attacked so that the mark you were supposed to leave, your signature, will always be bruised. Imagine the most extraordinary people in the world walking with brokenness, the most incredible people in the world believing the greatest illusion that they are not great. When you sit with this, you'll begin to see the unadulterated truth. Once you see it and believe in it, nothing can take that away from you.

Now, what do we do? Every one of us has teachers. We talk about those teachers who come into our lives that make us feel unworthy. Those teachers that we marry. Those teachers that we work with on the job. What do I mean by that? A teacher is the one person in your world who aggravates you the most. A teacher is that person assigned to you that comes to wake you up to the truth. The teachers began to show up ever since you adopted the false belief about yourself. So, look around at who aggravates you the most right now. Do yourself a favor and write down what they do.

QUESTION:

How does the person who irritates you the most make you feel?

Write down all of those words. Do they make you feel less than your worth? Do they make you feel rejected? Do they make you think that you're not good enough? I want you to think of everything you can and jot it down. Now, after you jot down the teacher, I want you to flip those words around. Turn not good enough into good enough—the unworthy into worthy, the forsaken into remembered, and you're going to see that the same words you wrote down reflect the atmosphere that everyone sees on you. Did you hear me correctly? I said that the people that aggravate you, not those who pat you on the back, not the ones who made you feel like you could do anything, but the people who put you through a place called Hell are the very people that came in your life to wake you up to the truth. So, look at the anger that you're carrying toward these teachers. Remember, teachers repeat themselves. They show up repeatedly in different forms because life will not release you from the teachers until you wake up to the truth. When it's time for you to wake up, you must have acquired the knowledge to understand that story.

When you realize the truth, you'll understand why each teacher was there. You'll understand why that husband, why that abuser was there. That person was there to wake you up. It works like this, one day, you walk to your room and say to yourself, "I'm better than how they're treating me. I am better, and I will not tolerate it anymore." The day that you do this is the day that you wake up to a truth. Most people don't have the skills or tools to wake up, so they go back into toxic relationships. They get rid of one negative person and get into a relationship with the next teacher, and this teacher does the same thing. If you ever want to get rid of a teacher, listen to what I'm telling you. When the teacher points you to the atmosphere, embrace it. This is the point where you lay down at night and talk to spirit. This is the time when you call these teachers to you. You call them to you and say, "I know you didn't choose me for the basketball team. The reason you didn't choose me for the basketball team was because God had already chosen me for His team." When you see that truth where you have God backing you, you can begin to look at each teacher. Another example is that person who made you feel like everything you ever did wasn't good enough. Now you go to that teacher where it first started. You say this, "It would never be good enough for you, but it's good enough for me, and I should never have let you determine my worth." These are the things, my friend, that you must go back and talk to the inner child about because the inner child is still frozen in the moment that you walked away. When you began to feel unworthy, when people turned their backs on you, you started the process of turning your back on yourself. So, this is where you go to the little child and get some things straight.

I want you to see yourself sitting in the chair. I want you to see yourself on your most hurt day. That day when everything went wrong. I want you to walk up to that little child and listen to what that child says. He says, "They just forgot about me. They overlooked me like I wasn't even there." Most people will have trouble talking to the inner child about these issues because they haven't solved a problem in their day as of yet. The truth shall not only set the little child free, but it will set you free also. So, when you go back, you look at the child and tell them the truth. When in doubt, point to the atmosphere. When discouraged, point to the atmosphere. When you're talking to the child, look at the atmosphere, and remind the child of who he is. Tell that little child sitting in that chair that because of the mark, because of the gift that you're carrying, you have to go through some trials and tribulations. Because of the gift you possess, you're going to have to go through some things. As you go through these things, never forget that they are designed to shape you for the reality that is yet to come. When you go back and follow this process with this child, you begin to free them. Again, I say a child is the most powerful thing in the universe because when you release that child, you begin to have your freedom at that very moment. If you ever want to see how a miracle happens, know that the truth will set you free. When you're free, your reality will begin to change.

10

ONE DAY

We are one. We had a spiritual encounter, a spiritual encounter where you walked up to the teachers and the people who have hurt you the most. The most powerful day of your life is about to happen. Now, you walk up to that teacher and say, "I no longer hate you. I'm no longer aggravated by you, but I'm grateful for you." Imagine being able to thank the person who hurt you the most in life. Picture being able to release the hurt and the pain that comes from a belief system that you created from which only the truth could set you free. Imagine looking at the abuser and saying, "Your hand didn't hurt" and looking at the person who made you feel unworthy and saying, "Through you, I've found my worth."

When you have this encounter, you will look out and see all of the people who caused the hurt. Then, you'll begin to walk up to each one of them saying thank you. Thank you for the pain and the lessons. You'll look over and see the very angel assigned to your life tell you that all the hurt that you went through wasn't for you in the first place. It was for everything that you're about to put your hands on.

Before you can walk in the shoes, you have to first walk in the story. You've walked in the story of the audience that you're supposed to help in this life. You took the polarity that you felt and found your crowd. In your atmosphere, there was worthiness, and you went on a walk of unworthiness. Your atmosphere was good enough; you went on a walk of not being good enough. When you went on this walk, you experienced the life of a hurting person. We often mess up when we try to keep and hold on to hurt that wasn't meant for us. You're feeling your target audience, and when you feel your target audience, there's a release that comes in your life. Remember, when the truth comes in, everything that was not true begins to dissipate. Now, what does that mean? You look at your child, and you say, "Thank you for the lessons that you taught me." You go back to your child and say, "I didn't turn my back on you, and if I did, I'm sorry."

You merge with that child, and the two of you become one.

When you and your child become one, there's an alignment that begins to happen. What is alignment? Alignment is when your gift, your purpose, and your pain all line up together. Now, what happens to a life that wasn't yours in the first place? Whenever one wakes up, that which was is no more. Whenever one wakes up to their truth, everything that the mask portrayed will leave. This is one line of work where the story may not turn out as you wanted it to, but it will turn out like you need it to because that's what happens when you wake up. Some people may walk away from you that you would never have had the courage or strength to let go. Some people will disappear out of your life. You may wake up and get terminated from your job, but you needed to quit anyway. You may wake up, and everything is over with, but it needed to be over anyway —and now you begin to line up with your truth. This is where miracles happen. Whenever there's an alignment, there's an agreement. When you show up in your purpose, the very things you prayed for that never happened will begin to happen for you. You cannot pray effectively wearing a mask because if life were to begin to happen while you were wearing the mask, you would forever lose yourself. When you wake up, reality begins to come into play.

Imagine that no one could stop the same broken people from coming into your life. Imagine that when you find yourself, that person that was really meant for you finds you. You were invisible wearing that mask. You had a fake life with that mask on, but the day that you take the cover off, the spirit begins to line up what it's been holding for you. Be the first person in your generation to have it; the first person in your generation to beat unworthiness. The first person in your generation that begins to produce seeds that are healed. Never have a seed until you embrace a promise. Never bring anything into the earth from this point on until you bring it in through truth. When you bring that child in, imagine that they've been born and birthed knowing that it's worthy from the womb. Imagine having a child born not having to suffer from the curse of the words "hard work." Imagine having a child who knows his worth and knows what to expect from this life. You, my friend, are the chain breaker. You are the person who can mend everything that's been broken in your reality.

Through this book, you were given tools to realize, tools to apply, and now you have to brace yourself for what is to come. Alignment means going to bed and waking up with things happening, and you don't know how or why. When you suffered for them and cried for them, it didn't happen, but now you find them coming into your life. When you're in right relationship, you have the correct wording. When you're in right relationship, you begin to speak those things that are. Why? Because you're speaking according to your atmosphere. If your atmosphere requires you to be worthy, you're speaking from the standpoint of worthiness. Therefore, God will not withhold anything from a man who walks in their truth. Scripture says, You have not because you ask not, and when you ask, ask amiss (James 4 2-3). What does this mean? Amiss means asking, not knowing the truth about who you are. How can an imposter have an inheritance? When your truth comes up, your inheritance is released to you.

It is said that a wise man will leave an inheritance for his children's children. You cannot leave an inheritance wearing a mask. When you embrace yourself, your inheritance begins to show up. When you walk in your truth, you begin to go and start that business. When you begin to walk in your truth, you begin to step outside of that controlled job, and become the entrepreneur you always dreamed of being, and when you become that entrepreneur, you must walk in worth. When you walk in worth, God begins to release things over your life. When things are released over your life, they are not just released for you. The same way pain traveled down that pathway; blessings are sent down that pathway. No longer are you leaving hurt, but you're leaving seed, and at this time, you create the family crest so that two hundred years from now, they look back and look at the crest and see the power of who you were. They see that you were an entrepreneur. They see that you stood a free man. They see that you stood a free woman. They see that you defeated those negative things that went down in your spirit. So when they look at that crest, they'll never forget who they are. Imagine living a life so powerful that when you close your eyes and die, a thousand years from now, you're still winning. The winning starts today. Will you lay aside every weight, every burden that so easily besets you? Will you be crazy enough to wake up to that dream, to wake up to your truth, and get the reality that you deserve?

THE END

ABOUT THE AUTHOR

Reginald Mckiver is one of the most sought after speakers, coaches, and entrepreneurs leading clients worldwide. With decades of knowledge acquired from being in the US Navy, a police officer and Special Operations and Response Team member, pastor, program developer, retail store owner, and founder of his own personal development school, Academy 333 (Academy333.com), he guides others on the journey to finding their truth and how to live freely afterward. He does this without judgment and doesn't hold back in his new book *The Baggage You Unpacked.*

Mckiver has traveled to over twenty-seven countries taking the time to learn life skills and gain knowledge from each culture visited. An east coast native and west coast resident, he enjoys spending time in nature, discovering new ideas, learning spiritual lessons, and gaining a fresh outlook on life and all it has to offer.

Reginald Mckiver is passionate about fulfilling his vision. What is that vision? Helping everyone understand why they are here, how to identify the mental blocks that have been holding them back, and how to take the gifts from those blocks and help the world. Since birth, he has been an entrepreneur and has been on several shows, including The Dr. Oz Show and various other regional and national talk shows —but all that matters to him is you. His personal clients include some of the best therapists, psychotherapists, actors, doctors, scientists, and the list goes on.

To learn more, visit his website at

Thereggiemckiver.com

9 781736 473900